Self-Care

calm Kids

By
William Anthony

BEARPORT PUBLISHING
Minneapolis, Minnesota

FUSION

Library of Congress Cataloging-in-Publication Data is available at www.loc.gov or upon request from the publisher.

ISBN: 978-1-64747-565-9 (hardcover)
ISBN: 978-1-64747-570-3 (paperback)
ISBN: 978-1-64747-575-8 (ebook)

© 2021 Booklife Publishing
This edition is published by arrangement with Booklife Publishing.

North American adaptations © 2021 Bearport Publishing Company. All rights reserved. No part of this publication may be reproduced in whole or in part, stored in any retrieval system, or transmitted in any form or by any means, electronic, mechanical, photocopying, recording, or otherwise, without written permission from the publisher.

For more information, write to Bearport Publishing, 5357 Penn Avenue South, Minneapolis, MN 55419. Printed in the United States of America.

Photo Credits. All images courtesy of Shutterstock. With thanks to Getty Images, Thinkstock Photo, and iStockphoto. Recurring images: Abscent (pattern from cover), ag1100 (paper texture), Puslatronik (font), Sopelkin (doodle embellishments), Amy Li (illustrations and doodles). Cover - Littlekidmoment, p2-3 - FamVeld, p4-5 - Robert Kneschke, Jaren Jai Wicklund, p6-7 - Evgeny Atamanenko, Irina Palei, p8-9 - kornnphoto, George Rudy, p10-11 - AnnGaysorn, Africa Studio, p12-13 - Monkey Business Images, ifong, p14-15 - People Image Studio, kdshutterman, p16-17 - wavebreakmedia, Evgeny Savchenko, p18-19 - Krakenimages.com, Dmitri Ma, Africa Studio, p20-21 - maxim ibragimov, Africa Studio, p22-23 - ESB Professional, wk1003mike, Nannycz, imtmphoto, Maria Uspenskaya, ryrola123

Contents

Healthy You............................ 4
What Is Self-Care?..................... 6
Healthy Body, Healthy Mind............. 8
Exercise............................... 10
Eating Well............................ 12
Yoga................................... 14
Meditation............................. 16
Mindfulness............................ 18
Positive You........................... 20
Calm Kids.............................. 22
Glossary............................... 24
Index.................................. 24

Healthy You

There are lots of ways you can keep your body **healthy**. You can eat right, exercise, and get good rest.

Taking care of your **mind** is one part of staying healthy. Having a healthy mind helps you live a better life.

What Is Self-Care?

Our **mental** health can change from day to day.

It's not just our bodies that can become unhealthy if we don't look after them. Our minds can, too. We call taking care of our minds mental health.

Self-care is something you do to look after your health. There are lots of things you can do for your body and mind.

Eating well is good self-care.

Healthy Body, Healthy Mind

Your body and mind work together. The way you look after your body can change things to do with your mind. It can make you feel and think differently.

Sleeping helps you get ready for the next day.

Exercising, eating well, and getting good sleep can help you keep your body and mind healthy.

Exercise

Exercise keeps your body fit and healthy. But exercise does something else to our bodies, too.

10

Exercise causes your body to make things in your mind. These little things help to make you feel more **positive**.

Feeling positive is a part of good mental health.

11

Eating Well

Healthy food is important for your body. It helps to keep you going. Your brain needs food in the same way.

Eating well means eating lots of different types of foods in the right amounts. It helps your brain work at its best and can even make you feel more positive!

Can you see how many more fruits and vegetables there are than sugary foods?

Yoga

Yoga is great for self-care. It is an exercise for both your body and mind. In yoga, you make shapes with your body.

Let's try cobra pose.

1 Lie flat on your front.

2 Place your hands on the floor near your shoulders.

3 Breathe in and push your chest up, like this.

4 Stay like this for up to 30 seconds. Take slow, deep breaths.

15

Meditation

Meditation can be tricky at first, but don't give up!

Meditation can keep your mind healthy by helping you relax and get rid of **stress**. It can also help you think about your feelings.

16

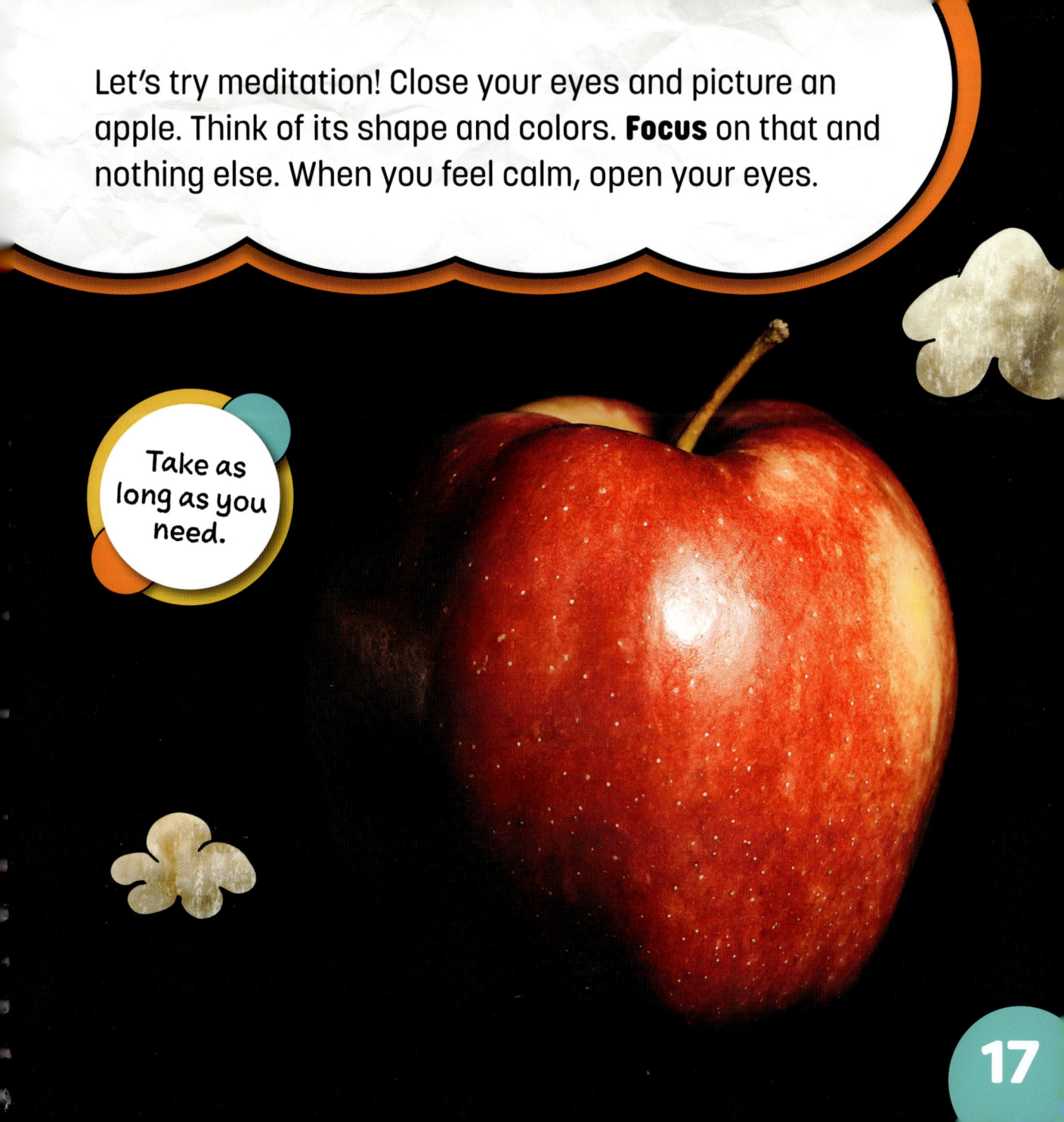

Let's try meditation! Close your eyes and picture an apple. Think of its shape and colors. **Focus** on that and nothing else. When you feel calm, open your eyes.

Take as long as you need.

Mindfulness

Thinking about the past or the future can make us feel sad or nervous. Mindfulness can help you keep your mind on what you are doing right now.

Grab a snack. As you sit with it, think about some of the questions below. If you start to think about something different, gently bring your mind back to your snack.

What does it smell like?

What does it feel like?

What shape is it?

What does it taste like?

Positive You

If we want to help others, it is important to take care of ourselves. It can be hard to take care of others when we don't feel healthy.

By taking time for self-care, we are more likely to feel positive. We can pass that on to others, who may then pass it on again.

Calm Kids

Self-care is a good way to keep our minds healthy and calm. If something doesn't work for you, that's okay! There are many ways to do self-care.

Try these things!

Go for a walk outside

Give yourself time to relax and play

Talk to someone about how you feel

Exercise or try a new sport

Glossary

focus   to give your full attention to something
healthy   when the body and mind are working at their best
mental   having to do with the mind
mind   the part of a person that thinks, feels emotions, and remembers
positive   full of good feelings
stress   something that causes strong feelings of worry

Index

body 4, 6–12, 14
exercise 4, 9–11, 14, 23
food 12–13
mental health 6, 11
positive 11, 13, 20–21
sleep 9
stress 16
thinking 8, 16–19